On Being a Bishop

Robert Burns
Edited by Alan R. Kemp

Hermitage Desktop Press
Vaughn, Washington

On Being a Bishop

Robert Burns
Edited by Alan R. Kemp

Cover Photo: Left to Right
Archbishops Patsy Grubbs, Roberto Foss, and Alan Kemp

Hermitage Desktop Press
P.O. Box 167
Vaughn, WA 98394

ISBN: 978-0692712870

Printed in the United States of America

TABLE OF CONTENTS

Saint Thomas Cross

Saint Thomas, the apostle and doubter, is believed to have begun the evangelization of India in the year 52, C.E. The Saint Thomas Cross has been used as a symbol of Christian faith in India from very early on. This evocative symbol has also been adopted by the Ascension Alliance and Community of Ascensionists, largely because it epitomizes a blending of western and eastern spirituality – with the dove, symbol of the Holy Spirit, the Cross of Christ, and the Lotus of India.

Image in the Public Domain

DEDICATION

This book is dedicated to the Most Reverend Herman Adrian Spruit, Archbishop-Patriarch of the Catholic Apostolic Church of Antioch–Malabar Rite.

In his ministry, in his episcopate, in his priesthood, and in his person he both embodied and sacramentalized all the choicest possibilities of neo-Catholicism.

"In those days, and even later, there were giants on the Earth." – *Genesis* 6: 4.

EDITORS'S NOTE

This book was originally written and published without copyright notice in 1980. The author was himself consecrated as a bishop by Archbishop Herman Adrian Spruit on May 22, 1980.

The book was re-printed by Sophia Divinity School Press on July 25, 2005 with a copyright notice. However, the book had already been in the public domain for some 20 years when this edition was released, by virtue of it having been originally published without copyright notice and because it was not subsequently registered with the U.S. Copyright Office within 5 years.

This book beautifully expresses an attitude of awe and reverence for the episcopacy–the office of "being a bishop." And, the author suggests that the new bishop takes on four key roles: teacher, pastor, liberator, and facilitator.

But the new bishop should also be wary, for the miter, a symbol of this office, is said to be lined with a crown of thorns. Status and honor come only when one has worn the crown of thorns and paid the price of dedicated service.

The present edition uses inclusive language, as well as revised text, some new material, and new photos. It makes use of CreateSpace and "on-demand" publishing, which has made it possible to produce professional-quality materials for niche markets, like the independent Catholic movement.

Archbishop Alan R. Kemp
Chief Executive Officer, Ascension Alliance
May 9, 2016

PREFACE

Arguments over polity and jurisdiction are as old as humankind, and part of the life of any human organization. It is no surprise, then, that the role of a bishop in the Christian Church continues to be controversial in the twenty-first century. Those of us who are progressive, liberal-minded independent Catholics have a particular version of this problem. We want to be forward-looking, non-authoritarian, democratic, and inclusive. We would also like to have a functioning organization, which might have a chance to flourish. In short, we experience the tension between the institutional pole of order and the creative, transformative call of the prophetic.

It might be easier if we would just call ourselves protestant, and leave the monarchical bishops to the historical communions. Yet we see ourselves as fully Catholic, partakers of the Holy Sacraments, and standing in the line of those who have gratefully received the gift of apostolic succession. From deep within the heart, our experience of the divine leads us to affirm the life and vitality of a Catholic vision of Church, a vision that mines the tradition for the hidden and mysterious depths of beauty, knowledge, and transformation. In re-imaging this tradition we seek to be both faithful to tradition and responsive to the ever-renewing Spirit.

Our starting point sees the office of bishop, then, as a divine institution that unfolded over time as the continuing presence of the Christ among us, the fullness of priesthood that becomes a touchstone for the ongoing revelation of God's presence and love among us. A little glimpse of the mystery assures us that our ascension to the divine absorption which is *theosis,* is also the profound emptying of the Self, that we might be vessels of the divine presence to the world around us—to humankind, to all sentient beings, and to the planet itself. Our priesthood is at its fullness when we surrender our own will to the divine presence *in order that* those for whom we intercede might be enlightened, healed, and liberated.

It is true that we often agree with the author of the Coptic *Apocalypse of Peter* who calls to task the proto-orthodox bishops and deacons for being empty wells, and lifeless "dry canals." Yet our rejection of the monarchy and patriarchy of what is termed the Kyriachal Church is more than just a cry of protest and reformation, it is a challenge to ourselves and others to radically open ourselves to the sending out of the Spirit, to renew the face of the earth. (Ps. 104:30)

This little book is a hidden gem of the wisdom and consciousness that has come through the independent Catholic experience of the 20th and 21st centuries. It teaches us both how to be a bishop and how not to be a bishop. If we can even open our hearts a little bit, we will fulfill the teaching of Jesus who said, "The greatest among you will be your servant." (Mt. 23:11)

Mar Roberto de Los Angeles Foss
Presiding Bishop, Ascension Alliance
Pentecost Sunday, 2016

FOREWORD

When I began my journey into Independent Catholicism in the early 1980's I was fascinated by the beauty of the Mass. The bishops and priests at the altar created a holy dance dressed in different colors depending on the liturgical season. The bishops were set apart by the miter they wore, the crozier in their hand, and ring on their fingers. They seemed to "anchor" the energy of the Mass. I thought that the person appointed to this Holy office had to be called of God and possess qualities of great spiritual value. In this book, "On Being a Bishop", Robert Burns confirms this and more. "Episcopacy once humbly received as God's gift is also, and must be, a skill to be mastered."

We learn practical things to do and attitudes, which work to fulfill the Bishop's functions as a Teacher, a Pastor, a Liberator, and a Facilitator. We get insight on how to liberate His people from the chaos of today's world. For example, providing pastoral care to the people of God requires a life dedicated to perpetual care of the bishop's own connection to the Divine. For only in this way can a Bishop give a touch, a glance, a word, to lift the oppressed soul toward liberation.

Other nuggets of wisdom are sprinkled throughout, like, "A Bishop teaches Christ, not Church" and "Ministry is based first and foremost on listening." In this way, a bishop must also be a Christian Mystic, timely, instantaneous, and eternal, all combined outside of time to view things as God sees them–eternity in a single moment. As a Facilitator, having a mystical understanding, thorough knowledge, and practice with the Sacraments will assist the Bishop in helping his people in their search to find the face of God, and the Bishop to understand why he or she has been called to this Holy and Sacred office.

Imbibe the teachings of this book, and it will give you the tools with which to experience the fullness and glory of the Episcopate.

Archbishop Patsy Grubbs
Presiding Bishop Emerita, Ascension Alliance
June 19, 2016

PROLOGUE

The formula for a spiritually successful episcopacy is so simple that it has only rarely been tried. It has four words: teacher, pastor, liberator, and facilitator. The bishop who embodies all four is truly a high priest in the Kingdom of God. And, he or she is a living blessing to the people of God.

The episcopacy is a gift from God to the Church. God alone "makes" bishops; other bishops consecrate these new bishops, but the episcopal Grace, Power, and Charism always comes from God. And, the episcopacy, once humbly received as God's gift, is also, and must be, a skill to be mastered.

Bishop Charles Webster Leadbeater was among the first "neo-Catholic" bishops of the modern era. This image is in the public domain by virtue of it having been first published prior to January 1, 1923.

Bishops rarely have the luxury of ministering in Shagri La. Only the few can look down from a mountain top cathedral at a bustling world with a sense of being above the fray of daily living. The ordinary arena for service for a twenty-first century bishop is the twenty-first century–not the first century and not yet the twenty-second. The real needs of real people today–these are what the modern Neo-Catholic bishop must contend with. Complacency and lack of contemporary relevance are vices that sometimes afflict bishops in the more established old-line branches of the Catholic church, i.e. the Roman Catholic Church (bodies in communion with the Bishop of Rome), Eastern Orthodox churches in communion with the Ecumenical Patriarch, the so-called Oriental Orthodox churches, and churches affiliated with the Anglican Communion.

So, the bishop must be engaged and involved, as a teacher with the "real" needs and the "now" needs of the People of God clearly in mind. The bishop may, and should, draw on the wisdom of all ages when teaching, but it had better be focused wisdom, pertinent, and need meeting. Diffuse exhibitions of erudition or recondite knowledge may be impressive but the question always remains, "Do they serve?"

But, what is a bishop to teach? In a word: Christ! In two words: Jesus Christ! In three words: Jesus Christ crucified! In four words: Jesus Christ crucified, resurrected. In five words: Jesus Christ, crucified, resurrected, liberating!

Notice please, the chief teaching task of a bishop is not to teach C H U R C H. For too many centuries bishops have opted for Church over Christ. The result: rancid institutionalism. Our first predecessors in the episcopacy, the Apostles, taught Christ, not Church. Indeed, few of them could have eloquently defined the word. They did not need to; they were entirely too busy *being* the Church to squander time discussing polity, hierarchical perquisites or the menu for church supper.

The key to understanding how the bishop is to teach Jesus Christ, crucified, resurrected, and liberating, is for the bishop to recognize that he or she is a *Catholic* bishop. When the bishop has an open, free breathing, embracing, and holistic attitude, the bishop is teaching Christ. The bishop, by definition, must be daring, bold, eclectic, and enlightened in exploring every avenue, old and new, in the quest to find union with Christ in his or her teaching. "But, we've always done it this way," is not an explanation; it is an ecclesiastical excuse. Risk-taking, breaking new spiritual ground–these are the preeminent teaching tools of the neo-Catholic bishop. Tucked into this concept of "Catholic" is a universalistic imperative to dare all and risk all for Christ. And that includes fresh thought forms and new domains of knowledge, which were once held to be outside the Christian ken.

We should add a caveat here: bold, eclectic episcopal teaching is not a license to be either opportunistic or silly. If devotion to Kermit the Frog is sweeping America, no neo-Catholic bishop need jump on the bandwagon, to assure some transient popularity for profit. Kermit, loveable though he may be, is not Christ nor is he a Christ figure. Likewise, no neo-Catholic bishop is to be encouraged to teach personal "pet" theories of union with Christ all done up in quasi transcendent language if these theories are but a slightly silly residue of 19th century imitation Christianity. Cultivated obscurity is not a virtue. Awe is our reaction to God; it should not be the goal of a bishop's teaching. Producing awe-struck initiates has little to do with the joy, delight, and freedom of knowing Christ.

The neo-Catholic bishop is charged with the solemn responsibility of equipping himself or herself to teach. This means a life rich in the Christ experience. Having the ability to penetrate the mysteries of Latin, Greek, or Hebrew has zero bearing on living in the Christ experience. Touching Jesus in meeting others' needs; sensing Christ in the convergence of the universe toward its Omega Point; trusting Jesus; developing a hunger for sacramental contact with Christ–these are the learning instrumentalities for the neo-Catholic bishop.

Formal, structured learning, however, is not to be condemned *if* that education does not rigidify or calcify. Ideally, a bishop should be learning always and all ways. No bishop, as no Christian, is a finished product. By his or her example, the bishop should constantly whet the appetite of the People of God to learn. This, in itself, is a salutary form of teaching.

The teaching office of the bishop is different in kind from that of the pedagogue, guru, Zen master, or teaching artist. The bishop does not dispense "travel tips for pilgrims to eternity." Neither is the bishop called upon to hang out a shingle saying "Resident Theologian and Church Historian, Ring and Walk in." The bishop's role is not that of a communicator of "tid-bits" of data, nor is it that of savant and sage. A bishop may well be a subtle and enlightened guide through the realms of the spirit for many individuals, but such a gift is not essential to the episcopal teaching office. In fact, bishops, above all teachers, must be vigilant against lapsing into mere technique, no matter how "other worldly" that technique's methods or goals may be.

The reason: when a bishop teaches, the Church teaches. And the bishop teaches the whole Church, not just his or her portion of the People of God. A professor teaches a class and helps shape a culture. A spiritual master guides an individual or small group in ways of transcendence and frees souls. An artist hones aptitudes in students and shows a few how to see the vision at the center of the aesthetic reality. But a bishop teaches beyond the walls of a study or office or center or cathedral. The teaching office of the bishop is the "magisterium" of the whole Church. It is apostolic teaching. Those taught on a given day may be but two or three in number but the teaching is directed to the whole of the Christian Church.

This is not to suggest that the bishop is infallible. It is to suggest, however, that the Church as a whole is, and will be, preserved indefectible in Truth by the Holy Spirit for all time, so that even error filled or eccentric teaching is used by the Spirit as a negative pole, or corrective, to maintain the Church's bi-polar balance in pursuit of all Truth. This Divine Guarantee allows the bishop to teach with assurance and confidence. It likewise encourages all of the People of God to listen to that teaching with confidence.

Thus, without having to resort to overstated claims of absolutism, it is perfectly safe to say that the teaching of bishops is the normative teaching of the Church, as long as that teaching is of the Christ experience. When bishops stray beyond the communication of the Christ experience, they jeopardize their warrant to be heard. Even a cursory survey of history shows that where the teachings of bishops were found to be wildly erroneous or downright damaging it was because they exceeded their Gob-given competence by pronouncing on something other than the Christ experience. Those first twelve bishops knew better. They taught Jesus Christ, crucified, resurrected, liberating. So should we.

Archbishop Richard Gundry is the Patriarch and Presiding Bishop Emeritus of the Catholic Apostolic Church of Antioch. Those who know him also know him as a pastor par excellence. This photo was taken August 16, 2008. It is made available courtesy of Archbishop Alan Kemp of the Ascension Alliance.

The crozier each bishop carries, no matter its design or material, is a shepherd's staff. It symbolizes the task of pastoring. Any bishop who carries it lightly is a fool.

No more solemn responsibility can be undertaken by any man or woman than the ultimate spiritual care of the People of God. And no greater glory is open to a bishop. Souls, lives, aspirations, hurts, and hopes are placed in your hands. Ten thousand tomorrows may rest on a single word from you, a touch, a fleeting change in facial expression. The stakes are enormous. In your consecration, God places His People in your care. No healing or helping professional in our society bears such a magnificent burden. You, as pastor, do.

It was an episcopal trait in the past to approach pastoral concerns with regal remoteness or lordly indifference. That served to alienate. A second course resorted to by bishops was to drown their flock in a flood of words. Today, we know that listening skills are the key to pastoring. A third method might be termed prescriptive wherein a bishop would attempt to problem-solve by issuing direct episcopal orders to a person in need of help. That produced salutes, not solutions.

The contemporary neo-Catholic bishop has a broad and beautiful opportunity to reverse centuries of pastoral torpor on the part of bishops.

First of all, few of us have the care of unmanageably large numbers. This is a decided plus for pastoral ministry. Know your people. Know them intimately and individually. Other branches of the Church are now verbalizing openly the need for a more favorable bishop-to-people ratio. We already have that God-sent advantage. Each neo-Catholic bishop can be a model of accessibility and one-to-one compassion.

Secondly, few of us have to confront large territorial boundaries. We can be with many, if not most, of our people in a short time. Be where your people are. Be a member of every family. Prisons, hospitals, factories, courts of law, universities, homes–no location is foreign to the pastoral bishop. Worship and instruction may draw people to you. Love must draw you to them.

Thirdly we are not locked into a rigid system of pastoral care. We do not have to "process" x-number of Church members per day nor must we rely on a codified, pre-digested, technique of ministry. We are blessedly free to employ all modalities of helping our people.

Review these three neo-Catholic pluses and you will see they add up to *intimacy, involvement,* and *flexibility.* That, my dear brothers and sister, is the core of sound pastoring.

Seminarians of all major denominations are rarely late for their classes in pastoral psychology or clinical pastoral education, CPE, training. Seminary catalogs persuade the aspirant that here at last he or she will receive the real "low down" on how to help others. The newly minted minister or priest is then hurled into a parish setting and presented with a counseling schedule that would intimidate a group practice of psychotherapists. And early on the erstwhile counselor learns that the seminary catalog fibbed. He or she soon learns the definition of the word "amateur." A few survey courses, a couple of seminars, and six months of chaplaincy in a psychiatric setting do not a Freud, or Jung, or Adler make.

Some clergy never learn this. They cling to the potentially dangerous affectation of viewing themselves as mental health professionals. I have seen grave damage done by some clergy, damage that could only be put right by prolonged, truly professional, care.

Having knowledge about the dynamics of emotional life is an asset to the pastor-bishop, but we are free to avoid the trap of play-acting at professionalism in this area. This is, by the way, a great service to our people. Some years of experience in pastoral counseling have taught me that our help is sought not as mental health professionals but as sources of spiritual strength and help. Sprinkling psychological jargon into a counseling session impresses only the counselor. Listening with loving compassion is infinitely more effective.

If you are persuaded that an individual coming to you for counseling might be better served by professional help, and that person is amenable, refer him or her for that help. Know the psychologists and psychotherapists in your area. If you have reservations on the whole subject of psychiatry/psychology, still stoutly resist the temptation to tinker with true emotional disturbance in any of your people. A secure stance might be to refer the person to a fully trained counselor who is also a priest or bishop of the Church.

End every counseling session with prayer. The liturgical word, "Collect" means prayerful collection of concerns placed before God. Shape such a collect at the conclusion of each counseling session and invite the person being helped to share in that payer formation. Do not hesitate to offer the full sacramental approach to healing with holy oil, laying on of hands, blessing, and prayer. If sacramental confession is indicated, be so prepared. These are the healing instrumentalities of the bishop.

The challenge of pastoring for a bishop has two further elements, which must be discussed: guidance and defense.

The shepherd who permits his flock to wander willy-nilly over the hillsides is a candidate for unemployment. And so he should be. He is not doing his job. Likewise, the bishop who encourages drift or allows factionalism or tolerates petty tyranny by certain individuals in his or her group is not discharging the pastoral responsibility. Cohesion is not a luxury to a small group; is an absolute necessity if there is to be genuine sharing and a chance for growth. Assuring such cohesion is the bishop's pastoral duty.

Loving persuasion and consistent concern by the bishop usually are sufficient to insure a sense of community in a group. Active and living liturgical and sacramental worship is a sure unitizing element. But, on occasion, it has not been unknown that a bishop needed to resort to gentle rebuke and Apostolic firmness to bind the group closer together in shared commitment to common goals. It was a technique employed in His pastoral ministry by Jesus. The lesson is well taken.

Under this heading of guidance, in addition to uniting one's group, the bishop is also called upon to give his or her group direction. It is the bishop, no matter how well advised, who bears final responsibility for charting his or her group's course. The bishop sets the agenda for spiritual growth. No neo-Catholic bishop cannot afford to be a custodian; he or she must be a scout, an explorer, a trail blazer. So, the bishop must be a source of fresh ideas, renewed hopes, penny-bright challenges. Here the imagery of the shepherd breaks down. Shepherds guide from behind the flock. The bishop must ride point, out in front of the group, summoning, beckoning, inviting. A private prayer for energy and vision should be on the lips of every bishop, every day.

Caring ... Guiding ... Defending.

Our shepherd friend must be vigilant at all times to protect the flock. The same task is incumbent upon a bishop.

We live in a society about ready to flex its muscles in the directions of religion. The challenge of being a Christian may one day be a bit more costly than it has been. Despite Constitutional guarantees, religion is fast approaching the status of becoming another government-regulated industry. Significantly, St. Luke wrote the Acts of the Apostles in order to persuade the governmental authorities of the Roman Empire to accord Christianity the rank of "religio licita," a legally correct sect permitted to publicly exist by the state. His effort failed, thank God. Christianity once again has fallen into the category of "religio licita" here in America, a tolerated and much regulated "sect."

The neo-Catholic bishop must be alert and bold in defending his or her group from predatory bureaucrats who like their religion served neat and simple. Federal, state, and local functionaries have a bewildering array of annoyances available to them with which to shake and disturb small groups. The bishop stands between his or her flock and these new Caesars.

So, too, must the bishop be poised to defend the group against merchants of religious quackery who would just love to cast a recruiting net among your people. Identify them to your people. Shine the bright light of your episcopal teaching on them. That portion of the People of God entrusted to your care is a sacred trust to be protected.

That crozier you hold in your left hand, by Brothers and Sisters, symbolizes caring, guidance, and defense. Jesus, the Good Shepherd, is our model. Learn from Him.

LIBERATOR

During the 1980s and early 90s a violent civil war raged in El Salvador that killed more that 75,000 people, caused another 8,000 to go missing, and nearly a million people to become homeless. Archbishop Oscar Romero is perhaps the best known religious figure and human rights activist in El Salvador. This photo of a mural in El Salvador recalls Romero's role in exposing injustice. It is made available by Alison McKellar under Creative Commons Attribution 2.0 Generic License.

That bishop who does not envision himself or herself as a revolutionary is making a major miscalculation.

The 21st Century neo-Catholic bishop is called upon to be a liberator, a true table-turner in the Temple. That which we are challenged to toss and tumble is the tyranny of time: the past, the present, and the future.

Each modern neo-Catholic bishop must handle the past with care. Seek out the treasures hidden in yesterday and bring them to your people. But the past is valuable only in its application to today's needs. Learn from it but never worship it. The Church is not its history. Christ is now. You must be prepared to free, to unshackle your people from the dead weight of too many yesterdays, which appear venerable in the afterglow of history. Many will come to you laden with dead questions from the past. Show them *now*. Invite them into tomorrow.

Let me share an example with you. The Christological issues allegedly settled at the first ecumenical council at Nicea, in 325, C.E. are drummed into the theological student until he or she is numb. None of this is a germane concern to God's people today. Yet, many of them are steeped in sermons and creeds, which hark back to the fourth century. They identify this irrelevance as being religion. You can, and should, free them from this by pointing to the Christ-experience as being real and present for them. The bishop is the liberator.

A Confession is in order here. I am addicted to the study of Church history. When I first entered into parochial ministry, I eagerly awaited questions on the first seven ecumenical councils, the anti-popes, the decrees of Trent and Vatican I and II. The questions never came. The People of God seek Christ in their lives. And they know that unless Christ is of today, they must go elsewhere.

During my training, I toiled for two years as an assistant to a parish priest who was celebrated for his towering intellect. His Sunday sermons were tours de force of biblical knowledge, careful analysis of ancient texts in three languages, and brilliant synopses of obscure incidents in Hebrew and Christian history. Week in and week out his parishioners were dazzled by these pyrotechnics of the mind. One day he resigned his cure to take advantage of scholarship opportunity to study 8th and 9th century theology. Now came the real test of his years of pulpit punditry. Had these sermons, so rich in the lore of the past supplied sufficient sustenance to hold his people together in his absence? The facts are these: the parish virtually disintegrated, snarling in-fighting began, and the Church school, once 120 strong, shrank to eight students. Instead of communicating Christ to his people, this priest had been content to feed them on the past. Christ supplies continuity and growth; Christ nourishes. The past is the spiritual diet of Jello–bright, colorful, shimmering–but powerless to sustain real people.

In your ministry you will encounter searching souls who are still encumbered by a Christian rearing which focused almost exclusively on yesterday's issues. They will speak to you in code. Baptismal regeneration, indulgences, being slain in the Spirit, purgatory, prevenient grace, predestination, *trans*-substantiation, *con*-substantiation–it goes on and on. No matter the denominational source, thousands upon thousands of questing Christians have been taught this ecclesiastical Esperanto as a substitute for the Christian's native tongue, the language of love. It will be your task to effectively liberate them from this spiritual dead weight.

And, not only must the neo-Catholic bishop stand ready to release his or her people from the church-y past, he or she will also be called upon to free them from portions of their personal past. It is a lamentable, but demonstrable, truth that the Church, both Catholic and Protestant, for too many years lubricated the engine of merchandized salvation with the oil of guilt. Someone once said that the surest way to commercial success is to create a need and then be the only store in town that can meet that need. That served as the working axiom for the Church for so long. Sin, guilt, punishment, wrath and vengeance became the stock of Christian commodities. And otherwise rational and decent people became convinced that unless they returned each week for regular refills of condemnatory oratory or confessional cleansing they would face a harsh judgment both here and hereafter.

Much of that dreary music has ceased in the Church but the melody lingers on in individual souls who, no matter how sophisticated or mature, cannot shake this guilt formation reflex implanted in them since their youth. They will need your liberating help. "Neither do I condemn you," said Jesus. Your people want to hear those same words spoken authoritatively and meaningfully in their lives by their bishop, by you. Your liberating gentleness can spell personal freedom for people who have been cruelly manipulated by guilt. Many are wary of any church experience precisely because of this. As you give them the gift of lightness of spirit you will help to work a personal revolution in their lives. You will be a Bishop-Liberator.

If the past must be challenged by the bishop, so must the present. You will be ministering to people who live in a society, which has fed them on a steady diet of illusion, appearances, so called "facts," and told them that this was the recipe for "reality." For a bedtime snack, our culture serves them a steaming helping of escapism. People will come to you secure in the belief that they live in "the real world," which is made up of cavities, crab grass, bills, taxes, nine-to-five jobs, freeway traffic, and TV commercials. Their clock radios are their hymn to a new day and late night talk hosts are their "Now I lay me down to sleep" prayers. What transpires in between, the daily present is allegedly "reality."

At first, you will seem like Don Quixote to them when you suggest forcefully that they are really alive on several levels simultaneously and that their spirit-selves are confronting more reality in a micro-second than their somatic selves deal with in an average work week. As you open to them the rich reality of their lives in Christ, they may be initially resistant. Soon, however, it will become clear that you are not preaching "pie-in-the-sky-bye-and-bye" but rather "The Power of Christ's Love is *Here and Now*." You will be freeing them from the fascism of "facts," the tyranny of appearances, the dictatorship of illusion and introducing them to Ultimate Reality. Then, they will begin to see with new eyes and hear with more sensitive ears.

The word "ecstasy" comes from a Greek root meaning "to stand outside oneself." Great Christian and eastern mystics have taught us that the only reality is found in ecstasy wherein we stand outside the skin of mere factual appearances and enter into the core of Being. Pilgrims passing through this part of the twentieth century have been cudgeled by science, bludgeoned by technology, and mugged by the theory of a mechanical universe. They now feel like aliens in a strange land. They crave a path to ecstasy, to a reality orientation, which transcends the ordinary, the mundane, the accepted. Hundreds of commercial enterprises have rushed in to satisfy this need with everything from hot tubs to mood elevating drugs as if ecstasy could be bottled or sold by eBay or Amazon.com.

You, bishop, must be a Christian mystic. That is how you will liberate your people from the present. Bring them into the ecstasy of the Christ-experience.

The past … the present … and the future.

There is a white-steepled church in our town, which is known for its billboard slogans. Last week's read: "Make a Down Payment on Your Future: Come to Church on Sunday." I and one of my priests nearly met our future when we drove by and read the sign. We began laughing so hard we nearly merged our Plymouth with the brick façade of the church building. Those twelve words on that church bulletin board sum up some of the worst Christian thinking available today. If you change the last five words to say "Buy a Plot This Week" the sign could well hang outside of Forest Lawn Cemetery.

Christianity has long marketed a quaint and deadly doctrine that heave is a future-place and religion is a pay-as-you-go installment plan approach to getting there. This kept a pliant people in their pews and the church's coffers full. Too bad it is a lie.

Heaven, dear brothers and sisters, is *Now*. Heaven is a state of being, not a place. Detroit is a place. And Christianity is not a travel agency booking tours to some celestial Disneyland. St. Paul, in a moment of ecstasy, was granted entrance to heaven and, articulate though he was, words failed him in describing it. This much we do know, he did not mention either Detroit or Disneyland.

Heaven is the Christ-experience, but it has an intensity no man can put words to. But, we have learned that the Christ-experience is what we bishops are about ... communicating it, living it, sharing it with our people. As you do the work God has chosen you to do you must be about liberating your people from the pernicious foolishness exemplified by that church bulletin board slogan. As the Holy Spirit works through your ministry to heighten awareness of the Christ-experience for your people, something wonderful happens. Heaven ceases to be a future-place in their minds and slowly comes to be perceived as a natural way-of-life for those immersed in the Christ-experience, for those who have been nourished on the moments of merger with Christ, which are the Mass for those to whom ecstasy is more than word.

God does not own a Timex ... or a Bulova ... or a Rolex ... or even an Ingersoll pocket watch. There are no clocks ion the walls of heaven. For God, all time is *Now*. God holds past, present, and future as a single moment. We mortals are the ones tyrannized by time. And the only liberation from that tyranny is to take a God's eye view of reality.

The revolutionary challenge is yours, bishop.

FACILITATOR

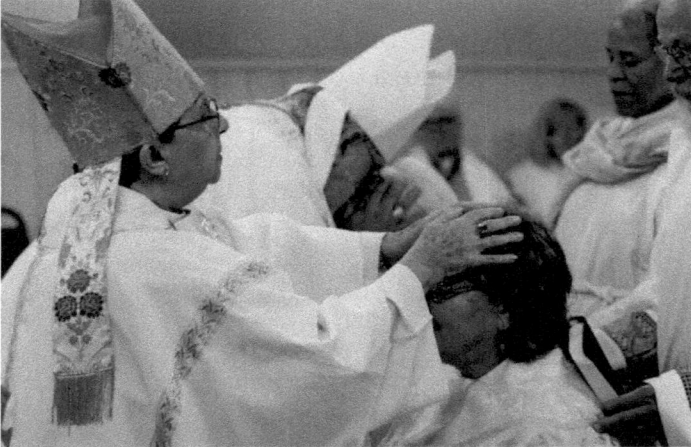

Bishops facilitate the continuity of the episcopacy by consecrating new bishops for the work of the Church of God. This photo was taken during Convocation 2015 of the Ascension Alliance, August 12, 2015. This photo is made available courtesy of Archbishop Alan Kemp of the Ascension Alliance.

It has been almost an episcopal privilege in the past to complicate the task of a church's people–ministry. Bishops have historically reserved the right to deal with "higher" ecclesiastical politics, to institute wildly redundant administrative procedures and to tend to assorted fine points of polity, vesture, liturgy, and program. Indeed, it became part of episcopal mythology that each bishop was omni-competent. Certain other branches of the Church went in the opposite direction. It became fashionable for bishops to cultivate the image of charming absentmindedness and dithering detachment. Both extremes served the same end: they made the bishop's office a dead end. Over the years, the Church developed a functional malaise; it acted as if it existed to serve bishops, not the People of God.

The original vision of the earliest Christian community saw bishops as having an important ministry, not a self-important ministry. They were not, and are not, supposed to be roadblocks. It is of the essence of episcopacy to help the Church to discharge its mission of worship and service. The bishop is called to be a facilitator.

If you are set on being a facilitator, there are certain steps you should be prepared to take. They are "The Three Knows."

First, know *your* Church.

The neo-Catholic movement is rich, diverse, and varied. Certain ecclesial bodies are highly structured, rooted in history, and exact in the rubrical approach to liturgy. Others are marked by a fluidity and variety of forms or structures, an anti-canonical stance and a tolerance for worship modalities other than their own. No one course comes with a Good Housekeeping Seal. Among the joys of neo-Catholicism is this variety. However, a commonality must run through the neo-Catholic episcopate. No bishop–Patriarch, Primate, Coadjutor, Auxiliary, Suffragan, Diocesan, Ordinariate, Peripatetic–can afford a merely glancing acquaintance with the structure, aims, history, constitution, canons or liturgies of his or her Church. Such a breezy approach breeds an undisciplined episcopate, a host of shabby ad hoc episcopal rulings and a confused people. And it contains the sees of a Church's destruction. The independent Catholic graveyard already contains many crosses inscribed with the names of churches once throbbing with purpose which surrendered to either episcopal vanity or a flip-flop attitude of "winging it" among their bishops.

Each bishop-to-be must devour and digest every official or interpretive document and publication of his or her Church. Each bishop-to-be must know not only the personality but also the thinking of his or her Church leadership. What is the locus of ecclesiastical authority in your Church. "But we are a non-authoritarian Church." Fine, but even that protestation is an authoritative statement, a judgment. "Our Church is an assemblage of independent ministries." Splendid, but who authorized those ministries, who set them in motion, what is the connective tissue holding the assemblage together? "We don't go in much for yesterday; our emphasis is today and endless tomorrows." Excellent, but who, yesterday, liberated you to take such emphases today? And why?

Does your Church operate under a Constitution and/or body of Canons? Have you read it or them– really read? When was your Church incorporated? By whom? What are its ecclesiastical antecedents? What are its lines of Apostolic Succession? Are there governing councils in your Church? What is the genesis of your liturgies and services? What is the rationale behind their selection for use?

The questions could be multiplied but the point is made. Whether your Church is highly structured or adamantly free wheeling, it is always more than it appears to be. Know what it really is. Only then can you both assure continuity while knowing with assurance the dimensions of any launch platform for change in your Church.

You may have no appetite for feeding on such detail (I will admit that, at times, it is the blandest of diets) but you are not informing yourself to become a Church Mandarin but to become a facilitator. Your ministry and those ministries which may be joined to your are made more effective because informed perspective helps any Church to be what it claims to be. Furthermore, those to whom you minister, clergy and lay, really do appreciate a bishop who can plug them into the larger purpose of their Church. Thirdly, such knowledge aids you to become a facilitator for the future of your Church. Is your Church to be a flickering, faltering, transient, footnote in the history of the neo-Catholic movement? Or are you committed to a permanence, an enduring witness?

This much I will hazard: those churches (and those episcopates) which are amorphous confederations of provisional problem-solvers who confuse the proud tradition of the "Episcopi Vagantes" with ecclesiastical freebooting will fall prey to disintegration, trivialization, and finally irrelevance in Christ's service. To the extent that a Church's bishops do not know their own Church, there will soon be no Church to be known. On the part of a bishop, ignorance is not freedom from tiresome detail; it is a death wish.

So please, know *your* Church. Know its "raison d'etre." Know every facet of its internal machinery, even if your Church boasts of having only two moving parts. Know its procedures. Discover which are most workable. Know every one of its ministries. And know its past as well as its prospects for the future. Know its personnel. Know its liturgies. Know a bishop's role in those liturgies. Know the full wealth underlying that precious five-letter word, "valid." Know your Church's spiritual heritage (believe me, it has one).

Facilitator or frustrator? The choice, Bishop, is too obvious to belabor.

The second of the three "knows" is: know the Sacraments.

Two steel cables bind the four branches of the One, Holy, Catholic, and Apostolic Church together: the valid Apostolic Succession and high Sacramentalism. The bishop is essential to both. By being a living link in the unbroken chain of valid Apostolic Succession; the bishop facilitates the Holy Spirit's work of sustaining and renewing the Church from age to age. Likewise, the bishop's profound immersion in the spiritual riches of sound Sacramentalism facilitates his or her people's contact with Christ.

No saint or seer has ever penetrated to the white-hot radiance at the core of the Sacraments. I (and this is a purely personal quirk) tend to toddle in the opposite direction whenever anyone advertises himself or herself as ready to deliver *the* definitive explanation of the Mass or the Sacraments. We are privileged to handle the Sacred. We are not licensed to explain It away. On the other hand, I revere those who lovingly approach the radiance and bring us back reports, even if words break and shatter before the Mystery. For my taste, any book, sermon, or tape prepared with this awe-filled attitude is always too brief.

The bishop has a dual responsibility vis-à-vis the Sacraments: to live as close to the radiance as he or she dares and to guard the purity of the Sacraments. The bishop/facilitator's role in the latter activity is what concerns us here.

The Sacraments are God-Man embraces filled with a transforming power, the Energy Source being Almighty God. Each should be handled with holy care. Assuring this care-full approach to the Sacraments is a bishop's solemn duty.

Elements within the independent Catholic wing have equated this essential care-fullness with rubrical fussiness, a form of liturgical Pharisaism. They act as if each Sacrament is a product to be subjected to quality control. The Sacraments are transforming processes, not products. Thus, I am not advocating a sterile Sacramentalism that is exacting but empty. The bishop's task is to take holy care of this great Sacramental trust. That means that he or she must exemplify, teach, advocate, and if need be, forcefully insist upon decency, correctness, due order, high spirituality, and adherence to sound liturgical norms in the administration of the Sacraments. If "winging it" is counterproductive in the area of knowing the polity of one's own Church, it is utterly life-threatening in the administration of the Sacraments. Whatever worship and service modalities your Church may use: *know them* ... inside and out, up and down, backwards and forwards ... *know them*.

As you teach and train priests in the Eucharistic Celebration and Sacramental Administration, do so with holy care and attention to detail. Share your love of the Sacraments with them. As you pass on the Sacramental tradition to junior bishops, do so with holy care and attention to detail. And, most especially, as *you* administer the Sacraments ... holy care and attention to detail.

I need not emphasize your august responsibility in exercising the power of your office in the administration of Holy Orders and the Consecration of a Bishop–Holy care and attention to detail. A thousand years from now a validly consecrated neo-Catholic bishop will cheerfully forgive you any excess of zeal you may have shown in point-by-point correctness of your ordinations and consecrations. Despite my earlier salvo, here I would not be uncomfortable with a bit of fussiness. Cross all the "T"s and dot all the "I"s. Do so and you will facilitate the future.

Know your Church. Know the Sacraments. Know yourself, the last of "The Three Knows" of the facilitator.

The one human being with whom I can guarantee you will work for your entire episcopate is *you*. It will greatly facilitate your ministry if you know yourself in all your internal harmony, all your potential, all your skills ... yes, even in all your limitations. Know yourself realistically, lovingly, forgivingly, gently.

Set rational work goals for yourself. Delegate responsibilities. Form yourself in Christ's image and likeness through prayer and Christ-centered meditation. Enjoy your episcopate. Stubbornly and humbly refuse to take yourself too seriously. In the Divine Plan, dear bishop, you are important; be content with God's recognition of your importance. And, to accomplish this personal program, you must first know yourself.

As you mature in Christ, those deceptively simple two words, "know yourself," turn out to be a key to catching the Holy Spirit at work. You see, Bishop, one day you will be toiling away at the Third Know and looking deep inside yourself when all of a sudden ... there is Christ. For the first time you will know yourself as God has always know you, as Jesus Christ, Crucified, Resurrected, Liberating. That is not identity confusion; that is Identity Completion.

EPILOGUE

Bishop, you are embarked on a journey without parallel. In you, the Apostolic College is enlarged and renewed. Your unique gifts count enormously in the shaping of the Kingdom

Have a fruitful journey, Bishop. Journey's end is ... God.

ABOUT ASCENSION

The Ascension Alliance and Community of Ascensionists is an independent Catholic religious jurisdiction and a clerical congregation–among "The Other Catholics." As such, we are part of a spiritual movement and of the one Mystical Body of Christ: a Church; a religious jurisdiction; an umbrella organization; and an expression of God's mystical movement of Spirit. We draw our lineage, or lines of apostolic succession, from historic churches, East and West, although we are not a part of the Roman Catholic or Eastern Orthodox communions. We derive our chief western lineage through the Old Catholic churches of Europe, which first separated from the see at Rome beginning in the early 1700s. Our principal eastern lineage comes through the ancient churches of India–believed to have been established by the Apostle Thomas, beginning in the year 52, C.E., and which were served by Assyrian and Syrian Orthodox bishops for generations. We like to think of ourselves as being born of a "free" Catholic (or universal) vision and a much larger stirring of Spirit, which beckons us to transcend old ways that no longer work, ascend to higher levels of consciousness, and be transformed. In addition, we are dedicated to helping other sojourners who wish to do the same.

We Joyfully Celebrate the Sacraments
in Communities Worldwide

Mailing Address:
P.O. Box 167, Vaughn, WA 98394

Website: ascensionalliance.org

www.ingramcontent.com/pod-product-compliance
Lightning Source LLC
Chambersburg PA
CBHW060632030426

42337CB00018B/3322